ATOMIC

GREAT ESCAPES

ANN WEIL

Raintree

Chicago, Illinois

Printed in China by WKT Company Limited

11 10 09 08 07
10 9 8 7 6 5 4 3 2 1

**Library of Congress Cataloging-in-
Publication Data**
Weil, Ann.
  Great escapes / Ann Weil.
     p. cm. -- (Atomic)
  Includes bibliographical references and index.
  ISBN 1-4109-2497-1 (library binding-hardcover)
-- ISBN 1-4109-2502-1 (pbk.)
  1. Escapes--Juvenile literature. I. Title. II. Atomic
(Chicago, Ill.)
  HV8657.W465 2006
  904--dc22

  2006004041

13 digit ISBNs:
978-1-4109-2497-1 (hardcover)
978-1-4109-2502-2 (paperback)

Acknowledgments
The author and publishers are grateful to the
following for permission to reproduce copyright
material: Accidental Film Company/Battersea Dogs
Home p. **26 bottom**; Aron Ralston p. **21 top**;
Camera Press/Gamma p. **6**; Corbis pp. **14** (Gerald
French), **29** (Dave Teel), **9**; Corbis/Bettmann
p. **14 top**; Corbis/Hulton-Deutsch Collection p. **25**;
Corbis/John Springer Collection p. **5**; Corbis/Reuters
pp. **10** (Hans/Deryk/Pool), **18 top**; Empics/AP
p. **13**; Getty Images/Hulton Archive p. **17**; Getty
Images/STR/AFP p. **7**; Getty Images/Taxi p. **22**;
Getty Images/The Image Bank p. **26 top**; Reuters/
Corbis - Hans/Deryk/Pool p. **10**; Rex Features pp. **18
bottom**, **21 bottom** (Action Press).

Cover photograph reproduced with permission of
Corbis (Bettmann).

The publishers would like to thank Diana Bentley,
Nancy Harris, and Dee Reid for their assistance in
the preparation of this book.

Every effort has been made to contact copyright
holders of any material reproduced in this book.
Any omissions will be rectified in subsequent
printings if notice is given to the publishers.

Disclaimer
All the Internet addresses (URLs) given in this book
were valid at the time of going to press. However,
due to the dynamic nature of the Internet, some
addresses may have changed, or sites may have
changed or ceased to exist since publication. While
the author and publishers regret any inconvenience
this may cause readers, no responsibility for any
such changes can be accepted by either the author
or the publishers.

Contents

Some words are printed in bold, **like this**. You can find out what they mean in the glossary. You can also look in the box at the bottom of the page where the word first appears.

GREAT ESCAPES

Sometimes people need to escape from a dangerous situation. This could happen during a war or a natural disaster. Escaping can take luck, as well as skill and bravery.

Harry Houdini

Some people perform escapes to entertain audiences. They are following in the footsteps of Harry Houdini, who was the world's most famous **escape artist**.

He escaped from handcuffs, prison cells, and locked boxes. His greatest escape was from the Water Torture Cell. First, he was lowered head-first into a tank full of water. Then, his ankles were held in place and the tank was locked. He managed to escape in less than two minutes.

escape artist	**someone who performs escapes while people watch**
natural disaster	**earthquake, flood, storm, or other deadly event caused by nature**

This is Houdini holding onto a skyscraper with only his chin, while wearing a **straitjacket**.

| straitjacket | jacket with long arms that are tied together |

A tsunami is a huge wave that hits land. Anything in its path will be washed away.

Key fact!

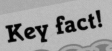

Tsunami means "tidal wave" in Japanese.

ESCAPE FROM THE TSUNAMI

In December 2004 six-year-old Yeh Chia-ni was on vacation with her mother. She was playing at the beach when a tsunami struck.

Up a tree!

Just before the enormous wave hit the beach, the girl's mother threw her up into a palm tree. "I was there all night," Yeh said. She was lucky to escape. Around 250,000 people died, including Yeh Chia-ni's mother.

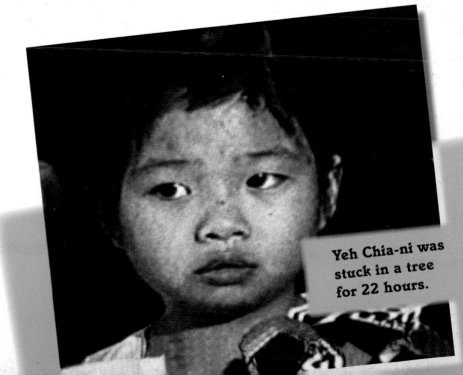

Yeh Chia-ni was stuck in a tree for 22 hours.

ESCAPE FROM SLAVERY

In the southern United States in the 1800s, escaping from **slavery** was hard and dangerous. Some slaves escaped on foot. They traveled north in small groups.

Henry "Box" Brown

In 1849 a slave named Henry Brown escaped in an unusual way. He hid in a wooden box. It was an extremely tight fit. Brown had drinking water in the box, and holes let in air to breathe. Friends "mailed" the box from Richmond, Virginia to Philadelphia, Pennsylvania. When the box arrived, Brown climbed out a free man.

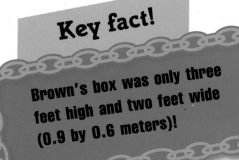

Key fact!

Brown's box was only three feet high and two feet wide (0.9 by 0.6 meters)!

Brown was in the box for 27 hours.

slavery — forcing people to work for no money. Slavery was common in the southern United States until 1863.

The fire looked bad. But everyone on the plane managed to escape!

Escape from a Burning Plane

In August 2005 a plane burst into flames just after it landed in Toronto, Canada. "We could see some flames, and that was when we got really scared," one passenger said later. "We didn't know if the plane would just blow up."

Saved by the slides!

Everyone escaped on slides that came out of the sides of the plane. **Flight attendants** directed people to jump on the slides as fast as possible. "You don't think, you jump," said another passenger.

Key fact!

Jump feet first onto the center of an escape slide. Do not sit down to slide.

flight attendant   person who takes care of the passengers on an airplane

ESCAPING KATRINA

In August 2005 Mike Spencer knew Hurricane Katrina was coming. But he decided to stay in his home in Gulfport, Mississippi, anyway.

Indoor surfing?

"The house just filled up with water," he said. First, he paddled around inside the house on a small surfboard. Then, he said, the water got too high. "It forced me into the attic. I ended up kicking out the wall and climbing out to a tree."

Spencer held onto that tree for his life! He saw his house crumble and disappear into the rushing water. Five hours later, he was rescued.

Key fact!

Some families had to wait for days or even weeks before they were rescued.

The rescuers came in boats and helicopters.

These prisoners spent many
months preparing their escape.

Alcatraz is now open
to tourists.

ESCAPE FROM ALCATRAZ

Alcatraz Island is in San Francisco Bay, in California. A prison on the island was used until 1963.

Disappeared!

Alcatraz's most famous **jailbreak** was by Frank Morris and the Anglin brothers in 1962. They made a **raft** to get across the bay. On the day of the escape, they put **dummies** in their beds to fool the guards into thinking they were asleep.

Did the prisoners' planning pay off? No one knows for sure. Maybe they drowned, or maybe they made it to land and began new lives.

Key fact!

The 1979 film *Escape from Alcatraz* is all about the men's famous escape.

dummy	object that looks like a person or part of a person
jailbreak	escape from jail
raft	simple, flat boat

ESCAPE FROM STALAG LUFT III

During World War II (1939–1945), 76 prisoners of war (POWs) escaped from the German prison camp Stalag Luft III. They got out through tunnels they dug.

Out, but not safe

Once they were outside the camp, the men divided up in order to not attract attention. Although they were out of the camp, they were still in an enemy country.

Only three of the men made it to safety. Fifty were caught and shot dead. The others were caught and sent to prison or work camps.

Key fact!

The prisoners dug three tunnels. They called the tunnels "Tom," "Dick," and "Harry."

Guards, watchtowers, and barbed wire made it hard to escape from Stalag Luft III.

prisoner of war (POW) soldier captured by the enemy

As the only POW camp with more guards than prisoners, Colditz was supposed to be impossible to escape from.

As young POWs, these men built a glider to fly out of the castle. The war ended before they had a chance to use it.

ESCAPE FROM COLDITZ

Colditz is an old castle in Germany. During World War II, the Germans kept POWs there.

Escapes take teamwork

The prisoners worked together to escape. One day, while they were outside exercising, six Dutch POWs snuck down a **manhole**. When the guards counted heads to make sure that everyone was there, other prisoners held up **dummy** heads to fool them. Later, the men hiding in the manhole climbed out and escaped. Two were caught and four made it to freedom.

glider	aircraft without an engine
manhole	covered hole in the street or sidewalk

TRAPPED!

In 2003 27-year-old Aron Ralston was trapped and alone. A day hike in Colorado had turned into a nightmare.

A life or death choice

A boulder had come loose above him and had crushed and trapped his right hand.

No one knew where he was, and Ralston soon ran out of water. After five days, he knew he had to choose: die there, or cut off his own arm.

Ralston used his pocketknife to cut through his arm. Then, he used a bandage to stop the bleeding. Finally, he hiked out to find help.

Key fact!

Even with his new false arm, Ralston spends a lot of time mountain climbing.

This picture is from a video Ralston made, while trapped, to say goodbye to his family.

Today, Ralston uses a range of false arms, depending on what he needs to do.

Even with skill and the right equipment, climbing is still a dangerous sport.

CLIFFHANGER

In 1985 Joe Simpson was dangling off a cliff. He had broken his leg while mountain climbing. He was tied to his friend Simon Yates.

A tough decision

Yates had been trying to lower Simpson down the mountain to safety. However, Simpson's weight was starting to pull Yates off the cliff. Yates, realizing he could not save his friend, cut the rope.

Incredibly, Joe survived the 150-foot (46-meter) fall. Then, he crawled down the mountain to safety.

Key fact!

Later, Simpson defended his friend's tough decision to cut the rope. He thought Yates did the right thing.

THE BERLIN WALL

After World War II, a high wall divided the city of Berlin, in Germany. West Berlin was controlled by the United States and Europe. East Berlin was controlled by Russia.

Risky escape

Some people in the east wanted to escape. But going over the wall was risky because soldiers would shoot to kill.

Some escaped by hiding in cars, while others escaped using tunnels. Two families even escaped using hot-air balloons made from sheets, curtains, and other scraps of material.

Key fact!

Between 1962 and 1989, there were around 5,000 successful escapes from east to west Berlin.

The Berlin Wall stood from 1961 to 1990. After it was pulled down, Berlin became one city again.

Red wanted to be free like these dogs.

One night, Red helped nine dogs escape!

A Dog's Tale

In 2004 dogs at an animal shelter in London were escaping at night. "We would arrive every morning to a complete mess, with dogs and food everywhere," said one woman who worked there.

Caught on camera

This happened repeatedly. No one knew how the dogs were getting out, so they set up cameras. That's how the workers discovered that a dog named Red was behind the escapes.

Red used his nose and teeth to get out of his cage. Then, he freed some of his dog friends.

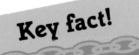

Key fact!

Red was found a new home after his escapes made the news.

animal shelter   place where unwanted or rescued animals are cared for until they find a new home

WHY ESCAPE?

Some people, such as Houdini, escape to entertain an audience. But for others, it can be a matter of life or death.

Bravery

Whatever the reason people try to escape, they all have one thing in common. They are all very brave. Trying to escape can often be dangerous. What makes people take such risks?

Some people who escape want to be free. Others must escape in order to save their lives. The decision to escape might be a difficult one, but sometimes there is no other choice.

Key fact!

In some situations, survival instinct will make both people and animals do things that seem very brave.

obstacle	something that stops you from doing something
survival instinct	natural feeling that makes people and animals want to stay alive

Throughout history, there have been many **obstacles** to freedom, but people will always find ways to escape.

Glossary

animal shelter place where unwanted or rescued animals are cared for until they find a new home

dummy object that looks like a person or part of a person

escape artist someone who performs escapes while people watch

flight attendant person who takes care of the passengers on an airplane

glider aircraft without an engine

jailbreak escape from jail

manhole covered hole in the street or sidewalk. Workers use it when they want to repair things underground.

natural disaster earthquake, flood, storm, or other deadly event caused by nature

obstacle something that stops you from doing something

prisoner of war (POW) soldier captured by the enemy

raft simple, flat boat

slavery forcing people to work for no money. Slavery was common in the southern United States until 1863.

straitjacket jacket with long arms that are tied together

survival instinct natural feeling that makes people and animals want to stay alive

Want to know more?

Books

✳ Borden, Louise. *The Greatest Skating Race: A World War II Story from the Netherlands.* New York: Margaret K. McElderry, 2004.

✳ Kulling, Monica. *The Great Houdini.* New York: Random House, 2003.

✳ Packard, Mary. *Ripley's Believe It or Not!: Amazing Escapes.* New York: Scholastic, 2002.

Websites

✳ www.pbs.org/wgbh/nova/greatescape
This page tells you all about Stalag Luft III.

✳ www.pbs.org/wgbh/nova/greatescape/history.html
Here you can find a list of great escapes.

✳ www.pbs.org/wgbh/nova/escape/strategies.html
This page tells you how to survive and escape after an accident.

If you liked this Atomic book, why don't you try these...?

Index